BE ELITE

BE ELITE

Climbing the Ladder of Success
on Your Own Terms

HERMIE BACUS

TESTIMONIALS

In the journey towards achieving our dreams, we often encounter individuals who embody the very essence of transformation and leadership. Hermie Bacus is one such remarkable individual. With no prior experience in the Life Insurance Industry, he embarked on a path that defied expectations and redefined possibilities.

Through his unwavering commitment and steadfast belief in the power of mentorship, Hermie Bacus has not only built leaders but has also guided countless individuals towards achieving extraordinary financial success. His approach, rooted in integrity, transparency, and the empowerment of others, stands as a beacon of inspiration in a world often clouded by doubt and uncertainty.

Within these pages of "Be ELITE," you will discover not just a guide to achieving your dreams, but a testament to the transformative power of dedication, mentorship, and a belief in one's potential. Hermie Bacus's journey serves as a reminder that with the right mindset and guidance, anyone can rise above challenges to reach new heights of success.

Prepare to embark on a journey of growth, empowerment, and the pursuit of greatness. Let Hermie Bacus's story ignite the fire within you to dare greatly, dream boldly, and become ELITE.

— **Haidee Collado**, Vice Field Chairman - FinFit Life

"BE ELITE" is an easy read and simple to follow. I am a living proof that I joined Hermie's team with no experience or background in the financial services, Life Insurance industry and in 8 years made over $800,000 a year income.

What I have learned under Hermie's mentorship has not just had an impact on my business but on my personal life and how I show up for my family and friends

— **Aneela Rafique**, Vice Field Chairman - FinFit Life

FOREWORD

I was honored when Hermie asked me to write the foreword to his new book, BE ELITE. I've had the pleasure of working with Hermie for the past several years. This experience has been both thoroughly enjoyable and educational as well. As the leader and head mentor of FinFit Life's Team Elite, Hermie has positively impacted the lives of many of our directors and associates.

Throughout my long career, I have been fortunate to have met and worked with some great visionaries in the financial security profession. I believe that I have learned from some of the best, and I can safely say that Hermie Bacus is one of the best. In BE ELITE, Hermie shares some of his most significant life lessons. He uses his personal story to teach readers about business, success, happiness, leadership, and the value of transferable duplication.

There is an old saying, "When the student is ready, the teacher will appear." However, in truth, the most exceptional teachers - or leaders - cause students to become "ready." The great ones don't leave it to chance that the student will eventually become ready, or passively wait for this to take place. Rather, they employ their talent, insight, and passion to galvanize such readiness. The great ones would rewrite the saying as "When a group has an outstanding leader, the team will become motivated, driven, and inquisitive." Hermie Bacus is that truly inspirational and gifted leader.

Hermie's own "rags-to-riches" story is not simply evidence that an incredible level of achievement is possible regardless of one's humble beginnings. It also serves to prove that when one follows an established system, has grit, and always does the right thing in the right way, success is inevitable.

In this book, Hermie shares his recipe for Team Elite's massive success. Success comes from exceptional leadership, combined with a proven system, the right dose of motivation, a caring culture, and the right corporate partner. But it's not just the recipe, the difference between success and failure often lies in the leader's belief in the system, and their willingness to invest time in training and developing team members. The final part of the recipe comes from Hermie's excellent moral and ethical compass. He believes in never taking a shortcut and focusing on the client's needs.

I hope this book will motivate and teach you to become exceptional. I am sure if you have any questions, you can reach out to Hermie and learn more about how his system can transform a new associate into a field CEO, quickly and correctly.

Sincerely,

Howard Sharfman
Founder and CEO of FinFit Life
Managing Director of NFP, an Aon Company
Chairman of The Finseca Foundation

CONTENTS

INTRODUCTION

"Many people who follow our system have been able to achieve financial freedom by the end of their first year."

— Hermie Bacus

The days of working for one company for the entirety of your 30- or 40-year career and retiring with a pension are long in the past. Many people now work for three, four, five or even more companies over the course of three or four decades—and coming up with your retirement income is solely on your shoulders as more and more companies eliminate pensions.

And yet, many people don't want to spend long hours working for a company when the only benefit is their take-home salary.

They yearn for the call of entrepreneurship, but the reality seems to elude them. For some, the idea is daunting, and for others, they've already tried to work on their own, but have not yet succeeded.

One thing, however, has not eluded you: your drive.

If you're reading this book, your drive for entrepreneurship is still alive. It's a goal you can't shake. You're driven to succeed and know, with the right opportunity, you could thrive as an entrepreneur. You're ready to give it one more try. Even though you know it's going to be hard, you're willing to pay the price and put in the hours to achieve success.

Road blocks

One of the problems that may be holding you back on your journey to becoming an entrepreneur could be your mindset.

You may think being an entrepreneur is something other people can do, but you don't have a chance. Or you may have tried to work for yourself before, and it simply didn't work out. Now, you may be afraid to try again.

While you know you want to be an entrepreneur, you may not know how to go about it. The choices may be overwhelming; which industry should you choose? What is the best opportunity?

Equally as overwhelming is the personal risk involved—will you make enough money to succeed, and how will your income affect your family?

Selecting the right opportunity is key to achieving not just success, but exponential success, as an entrepreneur. There are opportunities that offer linear success: you make one sale or work with one client, then move on to the next, and the next, and the next, making stepwise progress. Each sale or client offers a one-time revenue opportunity without the possibility of compounding growth.

But there are other opportunities that provide exponential growth. This is where the sky's the limit; your sales and clients build on each other, offering you a recurring revenue stream.

This is the path that can create wealth.

My path from linear to exponential income

I immigrated from the Philippines to the United States almost 40 years ago. I attended college and, for 10 years, worked as an engineer for the city of Cupertino, California. But when I saw the opportunity available in real estate, I got my license and sold houses on the side. I received a lot of referrals from both buyers and sellers and worked my way up to making twice as much money from my real estate business as my day job, even though I was only doing it part time. I worked both jobs for seven years until I quit my engineering job and went all in on the real estate opportunity.

I enjoyed being a realtor and helping people buy and sell their homes. Equally as enjoyable was the process of designing their furniture set up and envisioning my client's new lives with them, complete with a new home.

Although it was the definition of a fun job, and I made a lot of money as a realtor, it was not recurring revenue. People don't buy a new home every year, so I was always looking for the next client, the next home to sell.

When I moved into my current role, not only did I start making a lot of sales with recurring income, but I'm still helping people.

I'm making a direct impact on people's lives in a way even more fulfilling than serving as a realtor.

Along the way, I developed a system to grow my business, add clients, and continue to exponentially increase my revenue. Through this system, I'm able to help other entrepreneurs—like you—achieve their dreams of financial stability, of financial freedom.

The 90-Day Success Sprint: YOUR Proven System for Exponential Success

Through my company, I offer an incredible business opportunity for people who want to take advantage of a proven system to put them on the path to achieve success as an entrepreneur.

I have a comprehensive training program and a 90-day success sprint that can help you get up and running quickly. During your first three months, you'll go through the entire process of launching and growing your business—including licensure, training, company building, and client acquisition.

In this book, I'll take you through the entire process. We'll look at:

- Why some people have concerns about becoming an entrepreneur
- How to break free from the obstacles that may be in your path
- Finding your passion and motivation to operate your business

- How to go about finding the right opportunity so you can achieve success
- How to build your business
- How to scale your business for exponential growth
- How we mentor you every step of the way
- Why giving back is critical to your success
- A glimpse of your life as a successful business owner
- A detailed breakdown of our 90-day success sprint

Once you've finished reading this book, you'll know everything it takes to create a successful business that gives you freedom and a high level of income.

But why should you take my advice? Why should you follow me?

It's simple: I have a track record of success. I built my personal business to multi-million-dollar levels and taught hundreds of other people how to build a successful business of their own. Don't get tripped up thinking these people are "elite" or "different;" these people are of all sorts of different backgrounds, interests, and ages. You don't need a certain IQ to succeed as an entrepreneur, but you do need a system to get you started, and I've got one that's been proven time and again by entrepreneurs just like you.

So, let's address the elephant in the room: how much money could you earn following our system?

Like many other things in life, it depends on a multitude of factors, such as how well you learn and follow our system, how aggressive you are in implementing the system, and what your picture of success looks like.

Success means different things for different people. For some, success means having a five-figure income. For others, it's a six-figure income or a seven-figure income. Other people don't define success by the dollar amount; they're just seeking financial freedom. They want the ability to pay their bills, go on vacations, and enjoy their life free of financial stress.

What is your definition of success? Do you know how you can achieve it?

Many people who follow our system have been able to achieve financial freedom by the end of their first year.

Just imagine what that could mean for your lifestyle. You could have a nice house (perhaps more than one) in an upscale neighborhood, nice cars (think Ferraris and Bentleys), and take many nice vacations. You could even purchase a nice vacation home.

What happens if you don't act

Many people will read this book and not act on the information inside. They may think it sounds nice, but it's not something they could or would want to do.

And that's sad.

By failing to act, they're keeping themselves from the freedom and autonomy to live where they want, work when and where they want, and enjoy the finer things in life. These people may stay stuck in the 9 to 5 grind their whole lives, working 40-plus hours a week just to get by. They may worry about paying their bills, getting out of debt, sending their kids to college, and funding their retirement.

It doesn't have to be that way.

> *With our system, I can teach anyone who wants to learn how to become a high-earning business owner with a team of high producers.*

People who read this and take action on it could not only run a highly successful business, but also achieve an income and lifestyle they've only dreamed about before. They can put their money worries aside for good.

My goal is to help you, and as many people as possible, discover a life of financial freedom.

Let's get started to learn how.

CHAPTER 1

Don't Get Caught in a Trap

"You may first want to have someone help you uncover your true, deep-down motivation for pursuing entrepreneurship."
— Hermie Bacus

Don't give up—you haven't tried it all yet!

Many people on the path of entrepreneurship have gone down more than one road before finding success. It can be a struggle when you want to make it on your own and you've tried several things in the past, but they haven't worked.

You may feel like you're in a bit of a trap. That you've tried it all, done everything you could, and you still haven't achieved success. You may have read all the self-help books about starting your own business and being an entrepreneur. You may have invested in coaching or mentorship programs and you're still stuck.

You may have tried programs where you were neglected, received no guidance and had to figure things out on your own.

Perhaps you tried working for an employer, running your business in a traditional way, or attempted a career in sales. What about crypto or network marketing? Trying to start a business doing one or several of these methods may lead to frustration and burnout.

What about positive thinking? Having a positive mindset may get you on the right track, but if you don't keep up this practice long enough, you may not see success.

Yet, you know working for an employer is not the solution for you, and you're willing to pay any price necessary to be an entrepreneur.

But the issue may not be the effort you make; instead, it might be that you've taken the wrong steps—you followed the wrong path.

Don't become a saboteur

When some people think about becoming an entrepreneur or joining my program, they may inadvertently or intentionally sabotage themselves.

A common method of sabotage is poor time management. They don't commit to taking the necessary time to learn the program or learn about the product.

Other people sabotage themselves through their work ethic. They assume this path will be easy, and they don't put in enough hard work. Their expectations are in the wrong place.

Some people listen to the wrong advice. They may have friends or family members who own a business who will tell them what their business should look like. But since they're not in the same field, they don't know what the business should look like or how it should be run.

The biggest method of sabotage I've seen, however, is a simple failure to use the system. When people decide to do it their own way, they may rely on their instincts, and they won't follow a system that's been proven by hundreds of people, leading to their eventual failure.

The coaching paradox

Coaching can be a helpful tool if it's done in the right way, especially when starting an entrepreneurial venture. But too often, coaches jump in to fix the symptoms of a problem instead of working on the root of the problem.

Typically, what is the root of the problem?

Motivation.

What is your "why"? Why do you want to be successful? Why do you want to make a million dollars?

Coaches can try to teach you **how** to make a million dollars, but they can't tell you **why** you're making a million dollars. If you don't know why you want to achieve a particular goal, it may be hard to stay on the path to accomplish it.

Without knowing your "why", you may end up in the wrong coaching program and focusing on the wrong issues. You may first want to have someone help you uncover your true, deep-down motivation for pursuing entrepreneurship.

Most coaches are not there to hold your hand. Because they've never gone through the exact problems you're experiencing, they can't give you a solution to each individual scenario you may face. Most coaches don't even know your business.

In general, coaches believe it is their job to help bring out the best in people, not to take them through a step-by-step plan to resolve all their problems.

The coaching challenge for most entrepreneurs is similar to when they were learning to walk: their parents would hold their hands and help them. Eventually, they'd learn to walk on their own, and they don't need their parents' help anymore. The problem is, many students look for hand-holding the whole way rather than looking forward to walking on their own.

The difference in my coaching is I don't hold your hand—I give you a walker. I'll bring the best out of you, but I'll give you the walker, too. You'll be making progress toward walking on your own, not simply walking with assistance. I have a platform that will take you step-by-step through the system I've created, and by the end of it, you'll be *running* on your own.

What you can learn about motivation from a violin

A story about a violinist provides the perfect background for motivation.

This particular man loved the violin. Every time he played it, he was in the zone. He became a different person. He enjoyed it so much, but wondered why he wasn't a successful violinist. He was struggling financially.

He went to a coach to find out what he was doing wrong. After playing a song, the coach told him he had no passion, he lacked the needed skills, and he shouldn't play the violin. The man was devastated but took to heart what the coach told him, quit playing the violin, and went into business, doing things he didn't enjoy. He hated his work, but became successful financially.

After a few years, he went back to thank the coach for telling him he wasn't good enough and had no passion. Then, the coach revealed the secret of his strategy: he gave all his students the same feedback, because if they really love playing the violin, they won't quit. The man hadn't found his true motivation—his love of playing the violin—so instead of persevering, he quit, and gave up the one thing he enjoyed doing.

Overcoming a special set of challenges faced by immigrants

When immigrants come to America, they may feel a wave of excitement for all the possibilities available in the U.S. But there's a struggle too. There's a culture shock immigrants must face and learn to overcome.

I was so excited when I left the Philippines and came to America. It was my first time in an airplane, and I landed in San Francisco to this massive view. I remember feeling like I was in heaven. When I got here, I felt I could do anything.

I was living with my uncle, and he showed me around so I could get oriented in the area. I realized everyone worked hard. In the Philippines, there were no jobs for most people. With so much unemployment, people were either home or hung out in the streets or stores, doing nothing. I was shocked when I got here and no one was around. Everyone was going to work and, when they'd come home, they'd be stressed out and tired, and just want to watch TV.

After two weeks, I started school, and everything changed. It was not what I expected and that's when the challenges started. I thought maybe I shouldn't be here; it was so hard; I didn't understand my professors; it was hard to talk to people; and hard to make new friends because I couldn't understand them. It was a shock.

When I'd listen to people speak, all I could hear was "blah, blah, blah." I was amazed at how hard the language was. I was attending San Jose Bible College and wondered how I could graduate if I couldn't understand anything. I used a cassette recorder to record my classes so I could listen to them again in the evening. I'd listen, take notes, rewind and take more notes. It was a struggle. It was like taking the classes twice.

There was a lot of news about racism, and I started creating stories in my head, which added to the pressure I felt.

Those are some of the challenges immigrants face coming to America. They wonder if they can make it here because everything's new. The environment is new, the language is new, even the words people use mean something different. A lot of companies already have a culture established and it can be hard to fit into that culture.

The reason, as an immigrant, I thought I would have a better chance to become an entrepreneur is because I could have that freedom to be who I am rather than work for somebody and try to fit into a mold I have a disadvantage at fitting into, anyway.

After graduation, I worked for the city of Cupertino, California, for 10 years as an engineer. Then, I went into real estate. My ambition drove me, but I also wanted freedom. I got my real estate license in 1993 and worked at it part-time for seven years. By 2000, I had quit my engineering job to become a full-time realtor.

I worked in real estate for 20 years until 2013. I was very successful, made a seven-figure income, and had 15 employees.

But the industry is cyclical, and if I wanted to expand even just to the other side of the city, it would be expensive. I also found I was training my future competitors. When I trained an agent who became very good, they'd often split off from me, open an office, and become a direct competitor.

When you talk about the American Dream, it's not just about living comfortably. It's the opportunity to reinvent yourself, to scale up because, in America, you can come from nothing and still become a millionaire.

Then I found a better business model—life insurance—that I could build up into a true business that would pay me a passive income. It is the best sector in the financial industry and the best way to build a business. I could train people to become their own broker, and they could open their own independent agency, but I would never lose profitability. With life insurance, I could expand nationwide and even globally without ever having to open an office because I can run everything through our app.

I use a concept called Living Benefits, which was fairly new in 2013. It had been around for five years, but no one had marketed their life insurance products on the basis of Living Benefits. By marketing Living Benefits, I was able to build a business that took me from $0 to $1 million a year in income in four years. After seven years, my business grew exponentially. I was now selling $26 million a year in premiums.

Life insurance is the best sector in the financial industry and the best way to build a business.

As an immigrant coming to America, I faced a lot of challenges, but I was able to reinvent myself along the way. You can lose everything…and still become a millionaire again. The true American dream is the opportunity to help someone, to become whoever and whatever you want. That's the freedom we have here.

And that's the freedom I want to help other people achieve.

CHAPTER 2

Getting Escape Velocity

"The primary difference between people who are successful in the 90-day sprint and those who aren't is whether they follow the system."

— Hermie Bacus

The elephant in the room

It may not always be intentional, but sometimes, when we're on the verge of success, the people closest to us try to hold us back. It could be family members or friends, people that may love and support you unconditionally, but struggle with jealousy when they see you advancing beyond a certain level—beyond where they've settled for themselves.

It's a big challenge, dealing with families. Nobody wants to talk about this aspect of entrepreneurship, because it's an ugly truth, and it's always unexpectedly tragic:

Your family may not be supportive of your dreams and plans.

But it's important to remember this is more about *their* insecurities and not about you as a person. They want to keep things at the status quo. They don't want to feel bad about themselves, which may happen if you achieve high levels of success and, in their minds, leave them behind.

Another reason budding entrepreneurs don't get support from their families is due to a previous lack of success. They may have tried so many things before, but they're now the laughingstock of the family; who wants to protect them from failing again?

No matter what endeavor you choose, there will always be naysayers, so you need to focus on what *you* want to accomplish and not everyone else's two cents.

Challenge yourself with the 90-day sprint

My story is an example of how you can demonstrate to your family that you can be successful as an entrepreneur in this industry.

My wife did not support my decision to leave real estate and move to insurance and financial services. I was good at real estate, bringing in a nice income, and she thought I should stay with that industry.

So, I showed her my 90-day success plan. I explained to her that if I hit my goals in 90 days, I could duplicate the process with my agents. I can start by duplicating it with five agents, then 10, then 20, even 100. Then, I'm really scaling and growing the business. We agreed that if I could hit my goal in 90 days, I could stay with insurance and financial services. If not, I'd go back to real estate.

The 90-day sprint helps people focus on getting involved in the plan and doing everything they can to succeed.

Using my plan, I achieved my goals, and my wife realized it was a good move. In the beginning, I continued to work in my real estate business. Then, I realized that to be able to scale the insurance business, I'd have to give up real estate. So, I sold it and shifted to insurance full-time.

When I'm coaching people who are getting pushback from their families, I tell them my story. The first 90 days in any new endeavor are the hardest for most people anyway. So, this 90-day sprint helps them focus on getting involved in the plan and doing everything they can to succeed in those 90 days. If they really like this business, they have 90 days to prove to their families that it works. If their family sees the success they've achieved in 90 days, they're going to start supporting you.

30-, 60-, and 90-day benchmarks

It takes about 90 days to show success, and the 90-day plan I created for myself works for other people because it has easy-to-understand benchmarks.

For the first step, you get licensed, trained, and certified, then you start building and expanding your agency. Finally, you can scale your business by recruiting and adding independent agents.

This 90-day sprint is divided into three 30-day segments. The first 30 days is a fast-start promotion, where you may invest about 20 hours a week working on the programs to get trained and licensed. It's an earn-while-they-learn situation where you're already making sales in that first month. In the second 30 days, you're completing your certification. Then, you start engaging in sales activities and making money. In the final 30 days, you continue the sales activities and move into promotional methods.

In Chapter 10, we'll go over the full 90-day plan in greater detail.

Success, on the other side

The primary difference between people who are successful in the 90-day sprint and those who aren't is whether they follow the system. Those who follow our system have a different mindset. They *want* to be successful. They've decided to choose success and follow the plan instead of sticking with the old ways of doing business (typically, this would be people who have been on the traditional sales route).

With most sales plans, the goal is to teach someone how to be a good salesperson. With our system, I do that and more. I teach you how to be a great salesperson, but, to achieve even higher levels of success, I show you how to duplicate the system to share it with the other agents you'll bring onto your team. When you follow our system and show your agents how to operate in the same manner, you'll discover a high upside for growth and success.

Reaching the $1 million mark

I had someone on my team who was already successful in the insurance industry when he joined me. He had been in the industry for nine years and, at the time, was making less than half a million dollars a year. But he wanted to make a million dollars a year. When he saw I was able to make a million dollars in four years, he called me to find out how I did it. Because we're friends, I showed him our system.

Then, we compared our team of agents. He had twice the number of licensed agents as I did but was making half of what I was making. Even though he had more agents, I had more producers. His agents were not using our system and if people don't follow the system, they will not produce a lot. I invited him to join my company and explained he could be making a million dollars a year in three to four years. The timeframe would depend on how many of his people joined him if they were coachable, and if they'd follow our system. He agreed and, in less than three years, started making a million dollars a year with us.

This is an exceptional story of someone who had a license and a team, but once he started following our system, he achieved great success.

You can find that same success if you follow the system and stick to your plan. But first, you have to discover your passion, the driving force that will multiply your success in a fraction of the time. Learn all about what's important to you and how it will affect your entrepreneurship journey in Chapter Three.

CHAPTER 3

Enjoy What You Do by Finding Your Passion

"I learned a key lesson from my dad: 'Whatever you do, be the best.' You won't find your passion for something if you just do a mediocre job."

— Hermie Bacus

Be the best

I certainly did not grow up thinking life insurance would be my passion. But I learned a key lesson from my dad: "Whatever you do, be the best." That has stuck with me my entire life.

You won't find your passion for something if you just do a mediocre job. It doesn't matter if you don't like your job or if you even hate it. You still have to do your best.

I asked my dad how I would know when I was at my best. He gave me an impactful answer: "When people start asking you how you do it, that means you're the best."

That's why taking the journey to find your passion is key. I never thought I'd be in life insurance, but my journey took me from being an engineer, then into sales, and after that, to real estate. The tagline I used in real estate was, "helping families create memories" because that's where many of their memories happen: in their homes. It became my passion to help people create those memories in their homes. I enjoyed the process—helping them design their home, where they would place their furniture, where their things would be, and talking about dinners and their families. I enjoyed that.

I always wanted to give my clients the best.

Then, of course, I transitioned into life insurance. Because of my desire to help people become financially free, I really enjoy it.

Along the way, I always wanted to be the best, and I always wanted to give my clients the best. That's something I learned. When I completed the exercise of finding my passion, I learned I really enjoy helping people.

Today, sales are just a part of who I am. It's not even what I really enjoy; what I enjoy is the ability to help people. Now, I do that through mentoring and coaching people, but it may not end there. That aspect may continue to evolve.

It's a continuous evolution of who we are, and we should be open to that. The person you are today is not the same person you will be when you're making half a million dollars or a million dollars a year.

The late Jim Rohn said it best: "Become a millionaire not for the million dollars, but for what it will make of you to achieve it."

My passion is helping people through the products I sell.

Some people will say, do what you love, and the money will follow. Others say to choose something that people want. But that doesn't need to be the case. You can combine the two. You can choose something that people want or need and develop a passion for that by always doing your best.

In my case, my passion is helping people. But that's not limited to a particular industry. That's why I've been able to be successful both in real estate and with life insurance. For me, it wasn't about the product I was selling; it was about the result—about helping people through the products I sold.

How vision can take you down the right path

When people choose to become an entrepreneur, they need to start with a vision. What do you like to do? Why do you like to do that? Before deciding on your path, you need to discover your vision first.

Unfortunately, many people find a vision and later discover it's not what they really want to do. It's like climbing the ladder, and when you get to the top, you realize you're on the wrong ladder. So, to help people discover the vision that will take them down the right path, I have them do an awareness exercise—and they'll often discover that the half a million or million dollars are a byproduct of doing what they enjoy.

Learn what's most important to you by discovering your core values

Another area we may not think about because we're so busy living our day-to-day lives is our core values. Most people live their lives trying to live up to someone else's expectations.

Why do they do this?

For many people, it's because they never took the time to discover what they want their own expectations to be.

So, I have an exercise I walk people through to help them discover their core values.

First, I ask them to keep a diary or summary of their daily activities. I want them to write it down. I want them to track where they spend most of their time every day. Then, from that list, they need to identify three things: (1) the activity they enjoy the most, (2) which activity is required of them, and (3) which activity they could delegate.

When people discover their core values, they'll learn if their actions are aligned with their values.

Then, I would have them create a list of five areas: faith, fitness, family, finance, and fun. For each area, I want them to set a goal. I want them to know why they're doing all that activity.

For the next question, I ask them to list the top three activities they need to hit their goals in 90 days. For the final question, I want them to project how they would feel if they hit their goal and how they'd fail if they didn't succeed in hitting their goal.

I may also add an additional step, which is to get them to think about how they would respond if something happened and they ran into hurdles along their path.

When people go through this process, and if they're honest with themselves, they can discover their core values and learn if their actions are aligned with those values.

Several common themes have emerged. The first most common core value is spending time with their families. This could be their spouse, their kids, or their extended family. For others, it's spending time with their friends. Many people value going to church. Others value personal development. They want to spend their time in constructive activities. And some like to create content for training they're developing.

The key is to believe in what you're going to be doing. This lines up with the Vision, Values, Roles triangle. Once you discover your vision, align it with your values, and take on your role in the process, you can achieve success.

How passion can lead to success—even when faced with unexpected obstacles

A great example of this process comes from one of my top leaders.

At my first insurance company, she was making about $800,000 a year. When I made the move to my current company, she followed me. But there were a lot of challenges, and her income dipped. She was no longer making the level of income she had become accustomed to and lost her way.

She knew what she needed to do. She knew her core values, but her test had come. She was not hitting her goal because there were variables we didn't consider. We thought everyone was on the same page, but they weren't, and we had to make some adjustments. Now, she's excited because we looked at the situation, adapted, and now she realizes she can still be on track with her five-year goals by the end of next year.

Part of the issue was she had stopped doing the fundamentals. She was a top-level leader, but to reach her goal with the new company, she had to re-ignite her passion and perform like she did when she was just starting.

This is a process of reviewing and evaluating your core values that should be done every year during your annual planning. People's priorities can change, and you want to make sure your passions are still aligned with what you do.

Just pursuing your passion isn't the secret to success, however. In entrepreneurship, timing your opportunities is everything. Learn about the intersection between drive and opportunity in Chapter Four.

CHAPTER 4

Finding the Right Opportunity for Success

"The economics of life insurance are very different from what most people are used to."

— Hermie Bacus

Not all opportunities are created equally

Throughout my career, I have worked as an engineer and a realtor, and now, I'm in life insurance. I have been successful in all three endeavors, but not all three presented me with the same opportunity.

Many of my friends did not understand why I switched from real estate to life insurance since I was so successful in real estate and making a lot of money.

The number one motivating factor for me was more about the impact I could make. This was more important than the income from life insurance. I knew I could make money with both industries, but the impact I could make on families is more tangible with life insurance. I would be doing something that would have a direct positive impact on a family's finances.

Although I made a lot of money in real estate, I also lost it because, at the time, I didn't understand how money works. Part of the reason I went into financial services in general and, specifically, life insurance is because I wanted to learn how money works. I realized there could be many people in the same boat as me: you could be making a lot of money, but if you don't know how to use it or where to put it, you can lose it. I wanted to be the person that could educate people about money.

A cautionary tale about money

When I worked in real estate, I had a lot of money. We were saving a lot and investing. But we put the money in the wrong place. When the market dropped 50%, we lost half of our savings and retirement. Then, we took the rest out because we needed the money. We had 15 employees, and I needed to pay salaries.

Because I didn't know better, I took the money from our retirement account, which cost me about 50% due to the federal and state taxes I had to pay on the money I was withdrawing and the penalties I was charged for early withdrawal. We ended up losing everything. We lost our money, our house, and our investments, and we ended up filing for bankruptcy in 2009. The money went up in smoke. First, it was there, and then it was gone, just like that. It was devastating.

How moving into life insurance can change your fortunes

Although I was working in real estate, I did secure my license in the insurance industry in the 1990s. I was also licensed in securities at that time, but I didn't pursue it because I had my real estate license.

When I was younger, I was driven by money. I wanted to be successful financially and saw real estate as the answer. So, I kept my real estate license and let go of my thoughts about pursuing life insurance and securities.

In 2011, a man who joined my firm was making a million dollars a year. He re-introduced me to life insurance. But I didn't like the product or the culture I was introduced to, so I didn't pursue that opportunity. Instead, I stayed in real estate until 2013, when I found a company that has a great product I could align myself with.

Life insurance vs. other opportunities—Why life insurance is the way to go

There are so many ways of making money. So, I often get asked why I chose life insurance instead of any of the other choices I could have made.

When looking at life insurance as a career, one out of every two people is a potential prospect.

There were three driving factors:

1. Scalability
2. Paid Residuals
3. Time efficiency

First, the ability to scale the business is more predictable. Life insurance is not driven by the market. Instead, it's a need-driven product—and the leverage is *huge* for me.

There are over 330 million people in the U.S. Of that number, 54% pay a premium for life insurance every month. These are people who pay on their own, individually. This doesn't take into account the life insurance policies that are paid for by employers. When you include employer benefits, the number of people with life insurance increases to about 70%. That's a two-to-one ratio. And if you have a product that adds benefits to their existing policy, that creates a good market.

You can build a life insurance agency that leverages your time faster than any other opportunity out there.

When looking at life insurance as a career, you'll see that one out of every two people is a potential prospect. So, your success is just going to be dependent on how skillful you are in selling.

The second driving factor is you're getting paid residuals. You're building a residual income in the business, which is something you don't find in other careers.

The third factor is you can build an agency that leverages your time faster than any other opportunity out there.

When someone joins my program, within one year, if they follow the system, they could potentially reach the six-figure a year milestone. And they can do this on their own, without building a team. If they add additional agents to their team, their income could be significantly higher.

As an illustration, if someone builds a book of business up to the $10 million level, that could result in an annual personal income in the mid-six-figure range.

The economics of a life insurance agency

When someone enters my program, they'll start as an independent contractor associated with the insurance company, and they'll follow my process. As we already mentioned when we discussed the 90-day success sprint, at the beginning of the program, they're getting licensed and certified. In the next 60 days, they'll start the process of building their own agency. They'll be looking to bring in 30 agents to work with them. That's really adding an agent every other day.

As a new independent contractor, you'll be partnered with a certified trainer from my organization who will hold your hand and walk you through the process.

Commission-driven compensation

The economics of life insurance are very different from what most people are used to.

The way we design our compensation plan, the leaders in our company help everybody because they make money on every sale that happens in their organization.

Insurance companies pay brokers a lot of commission. They don't break even with a new customer for two years. The insurance companies pay for the prospect's medical exam and pay agents all their commission in the first two years. So, the first two years of premium payments cover the insurance company's expenses. That's why life insurance policies have a penalty that affects the first 10 years. If a client withdraws funds or cancels the policy in that timeframe, there are surrender charges. The life insurance policies we sell are designed for long-term strategies. We always tell our clients that if they're planning to take the money out or cancel the policies in under ten years, they're going to lose money.

When they hold their policies for more than 10 years, they'll make a lot of money because that's when they have leverage. For a $1 million-dollar policy, their premium may be $500 a month. After 10 years of payments, the premiums develop a cash value for them, a savings. Over 20 or 30 years, the return they'll make on that money will be a lot better than depositing that money in the bank.

For these policies, an agent's income will depend on the production of the broker. Insurance companies pay a lot of commission, so we structure our compensation so our insurance agents get paid well compared to other brokers.

For example, if someone builds a book of business up to the $10 million level, that could result in an annual personal income in the mid-six-figure range. That level of business is possible for someone who's been working the business for five to 10 years, and that's much better than Social Security.

Additionally, our agents will receive commissions on all the people they've brought into the business. The agent selling the policy gets the highest commission. As you go up the ladder to senior positions, the rate of commission gets smaller, but they're receiving it based on the volume of work of many other agents.

When agents are evaluating commissions, due to the volume of sales, the percentage of the commission they receive is not as important as the overall revenue they'll get from their sales. After all, when you go to the bank to get a loan, they're not going to ask about the percentage of revenue you receive from your sales. They'll ask about your income.

And this is recurring revenue. People aren't going to cancel their life insurance policies. Everyone is going to die, and they all need life insurance. We have a 92% renewal rate.

Keys to finding the right opportunity for life insurance sales

The most important thing to look at when deciding which insurance company to go with is the company's culture. Warren

Buffett did a great job of pointing out this principle. When he buys a company, he looks at the leadership. If he likes the leadership team, it doesn't matter if the company is profitable. If he doesn't like the leaders, he doesn't buy into the company. Culture is the core value of the company and its people.

Secondly, I'd look at the product and ask myself, "Why would people buy from me if they can buy it from someone else?" This refers to the Blue Ocean strategy, where you position yourself in the market in a way that no one else is selling your exact product.

Culture is the core value of the company and its people.

The third key step is the system you'll be in. Do they have a proven system to build your business—meaning securing clients and hiring agents? For this key, I advise people to be leery of any company that sells them leads. Because that means they have no system of generating leads or of training people how to generate their own leads. Without the ability to generate leads, you can't be independent. So, I warn them to stay away from brokers that sell leads because they're always going to be dependent on that company. They can never leave because they don't know how to generate their own leads.

When agents sign up with me, they have access to my platform, which makes it easy for them to run their business. Not only do they have access to my lead-generation strategies that they can develop for themselves, but they can also piggyback off my unique proposition, which makes the selling point exponentially easier to pitch. You should always be looking for systems that allow you independence and stay away from those that try to trap you in a cycle of dependency.

The final thing to consider is the market. How big is it? This is important because when you're selling something, you have to know your avatar and your target market. You need to know who they are, how big the market is, and how to approach them.

A bonus consideration, which is not as important as the others, is timing your ability to have ownership in the company. If it's a ground-floor opportunity, you have a chance of being a part owner or owning a piece of the company.

Now that you know what to look for in a company, scan the QR code to get an opportunity checklist and see which company I chose and the reasons I went to it.

The inner details about our product

The life insurance my company, FinFit Life, offers is amazing. It combines the two largest industries in the world—finance and fitness (or health and wellness). It's the only product that pays our clients for developing healthy habits. You're going to need life insurance anyway, so why not get an insurance policy that rewards you for having a healthy lifestyle? It's based on a point system. The more you exercise—and develop that healthy habit—the more you get rewarded.

We're rewarded for things we already do, like going to the doctor once a year, the dentist at least twice a year and getting our cholesterol checked. So, we're getting rewarded in two ways.

First, you can get credits or discounts on your premium or cash rewards or a discount on things you're doing every year. A routine checkup gives you 5%, which could be applied either as a discount on your premium or could be added to the cash value of your policy.

Currently, if you add two days of exercise every week, you can get to Gold Status, which gives you a 10% discount or credit. How would you like to get a $10,000 credit towards your cash value? Nobody else in the industry is doing that.

At the Platinum Level, if you exercise at least four times a week, you get 15%. Again, with a premium of $10,000, that would be $1,500. You could either take the discount or the credit. I don't like suggesting discounts because that doesn't help the client. I recommend clients take the credit so they can increase their cash value.

The second way clients are rewarded is through cost rewards, in which they can get a 25% discount on healthy groceries like vegetables. But this doesn't include beef or pork. They can also get discounts on hotels through Expedia. The amount varies based on their status. They can get a 15% discount on Silver, a 30% discount on Gold, or a 50% discount on Platinum just by exercising four times a week. That's a lot of money. That's thousands of dollars in hotel discounts.

They have to track your activity, so, for $25 a month, you can get an Apple Watch and, as long as you maintain your goal of exercising at least twice a week, you'll never have to make payments on your Apple Watch. A Fitbit is free.

There are also other cash rewards. Based on your exercise level, you get to spin a wheel every week and get $25 and $50 each time you spin, which can amount to thousands of dollars.

It doesn't matter what you're paying on your premium because it's the same program. Can you imagine somebody paying $200 a month, $2,400 a year, but getting cash rewards of $3,000? That's more than the amount they pay on their premium. That's the exciting part about this product, and nobody else is doing it.

Now that you understand the opportunities that will point you toward success, it's time to build your agency.

CHAPTER 5

Building Your Own Agency

"To work in life insurance and build your own agency, you must make the shift from employee or sales rep to entrepreneur. The best way to do that is by having a system."

— Hermie Bacus

Developing a successful mindset

Most people spend their working lives as employees. They work for a company, have a boss, and have a list of responsibilities. There's another set of people who come from the traditional sales world, where they work for a company and get paid a salary plus a commission. About 95% of the people we work with come from one of these two backgrounds.

To work in life insurance and build your own agency, you must make the shift from employee or sales rep to entrepreneur. The best way to do that is by having a system. And the people who work with us are given a highly successful, proven system. Some people who have gone through my program and use my system are making six- and seven-figure incomes.

To be successful, people need to shift their mindset from one of selling to one of helping.

The challenge for most people coming into our system is that they think they're selling. They think they're taking advantage of people by asking them to buy life insurance. The reality is they're only the messenger. They're giving people information to help them make good decisions on their finances. To be successful, people need to shift their mindset from one of selling to one of helping.

With the system I've developed, I can take someone from the ground floor, with no background and no experience, to the level of success they want to achieve. We just have to get them to believe in what they're going to be doing.

Most of the time, it doesn't take too long to make that transition. If someone is ready, it could be a quick process. If they have some entrepreneurial experience already, it could take them from a week to 30 days. For someone who has no background, it could take between 30 to 90 days. But it's important for them to go through the process and see evidence of success. That makes all the difference in the world. Once people see success, they'll accept the system.

The fast-start path to success

To accelerate this transition, we have a fast-start training program. It's a 30-day filtering process that lets us see where someone is so we know how to mentor and coach them. In the fast start program, some people will quickly move into the promotion process, while for others, it takes more time. Once we know where they are, we can help them along their journey.

This is why I built a culture where people can grow at their own pace. We do that by providing an environment where people feel they belong so they don't feel forced to do something they're not ready to do.

One of the reasons people have not been successful in their previous entrepreneurial endeavors is they get rejected from the company because they're not successful fast enough. The company essentially sets them to the side until they're ready. But they're not given any support. There's no system for them to run that will help them grow.

I've built a culture where people can grow at their own pace.

When I started with life insurance, it did not click with me right away. But I had a fire inside, and I wasn't going to quit. I sought out and paid for help on my own. I found mentoring programs, coaching programs, and other types of training so I could learn. But not everyone has that fire. They need help.

As I got into this model, I realized I needed to provide the type of environment where people could learn—personal development, spiritual development, professional development, and fitness. These are the things that make people want to continue to grow.

Embracing the skill set for success

Once we've addressed mindset, we move on to their skill set through a series of trainings I've developed.

I train my team on five skill sets that are required to be successful. They are:

1. Prospecting: ways to find potential clients
2. Presenting: making presentations to prospects
3. Closing: making the sale
4. Follow up: ensuring client satisfaction
   a. Building Relationships - within your team and your book of business
5. Completing the fast start: creating value and urgency

To help new agents complete the fast start, I've created a video they can use to present the fast start process to their incoming agents until they feel comfortable presenting it on their own.

Embracing the psychology of business and personal development

There are six steps we can take to address the psychology of building our business and growing through personal development:

- Meditation
- Investing in personal development

- Visualization
- Journaling
- Bookending your day
- Mentors and coaching

When I'm teaching people in my organization, I incorporate **meditation** to help them stay focused and clear their mind. Often, people wake up and start their day without taking any time to reflect. Meditation is one of the things that gives me more focus and strength and helps me stay grounded. This is an important habit for me.

I also suggest **investing in personal development**, but not just from one person. Following only one person is not beneficial. You need a broader range of teachings. When people invest in their personal development, they could double or triple their results. I always tell my leaders they shouldn't hold back on investing in themselves.

Visualization is another powerful method of personal development. For me, having a vision board is extremely helpful if I have a goal. When I was starting out in life insurance, I wanted to snowboard and teach my daughter how to snowboard. But I wanted to snowboard in style, to have a lifestyle experience, so I wanted the special treatment at the Ritz Carlton Resort in Lake Tahoe. I put that on my vision board and it became my focus for January. It provided me with motivation so I could achieve that vision. A lot of people put houses, boats, nice cars, and other things they want on their vision boards. It needs to be something that inspires you every day.

I know it's become cliche, but when you're serious about it, **journaling** is an activity that will help your mindset. I've been journaling for over 20 years and it helps me stay positive. Like Jim Rohn says, you don't want to get through the day, you want to get from one day to the next. Each day, you want to look at what you did, how you felt, what you learned, what you're thankful for, and what the one thing is that you could do tomorrow that will have the biggest impact.

I like to do what I call **bookending your day**. I know exactly how I will start my day and then I end with journaling. That way, you have structure to your day, and you don't feel like you wasted it because you know how to begin your day and how you're going to end it. In between is chaos, but you have a schedule structure. Your day won't always go the way you want, but if you bookend your day, it gives you a sense of accomplishment.

Personally, I start with the power hour. I learned this from Robin Sharma. It's a good exercise that helps me focus. During that time, I spend a minimum of 20 minutes on exercise, 20 minutes of meditation, and 20 minutes of planning.

When I'm looking at **mentors and coaching**, I would pick somebody because I want to learn something specific. For example, if I want to learn about leadership, I'd pick John Maxwell and read his books. Or the former CEO of GE, Jack Walsh. So, pick someone who can help you learn in a certain area you're focusing on.

Four steps to becoming a strong team leader

I believe in John Maxwell's approach—that when you lead a team, you need to lead by example.

First, you have to model it: you must practice what you're teaching. Secondly, you need to lead by experience. This simply means you have a track record of success. If people know you have achieved what you're teaching, they will follow you.

Next, you lead by empathy. It's easier to lead a team when you understand what they're going through. This can be accomplished by taking the first two steps: leading by example and by experience. Since you've gone through the same process, you'll be able to understand them.

Finally, you lead by empowerment. You want to help people feel stronger and more confident. So, instead of being a negative influence, you want to take a positive approach.

"Examine yourselves to see if your faith is genuine. Test yourselves. Surely you know that Jesus Christ is among you; if not, you have failed the test of genuine faith."
2 Corinthians 13:5

Building your core values

One of the keys to building your core value is to develop your heartset. Heartset is all about character building, self-awareness, self-management, and social awareness within relationship management. When you've developed your heartset, it shows your true character.

Because we work with people, emotional intelligence is key to our success. We need to master our emotions. We need to be aware of who we are and manage ourselves in our communications and our actions. I recommend the book *EQ Applied: The Real-World Guide to Emotional Intelligence* by Justin Bariso. It explains how we're all different, but we've got to know who we are because we all come from different backgrounds and have different influences, which help develop the person we've become.

Emotional intelligence is key to our success.

When you understand how you respond to people, your strengths, your weaknesses, what ticks you off, and what makes you happy, then you can manage yourself. For success, it's important we know how to communicate and how to respond to people in a certain way, not just based on how we *want* to be understood, but on how we *will* understand other people. That's having social awareness. When you understand yourself, you're more confident and more secure.

I think the biggest challenge for most people is they don't take the time to learn themselves, to understand who they are. Instead, we sabotage ourselves. This is very important; it really comes down to how much you want to bring value to other people.

I believe that we are all one, that what affects you also affects me. So, when I'm helping one person, I'm also helping everyone else.

The final factor to address is soul set and spirituality. When you have a cause that's larger than yourself, it will give you determination, will help you be persistent. It's the connection to the universal intelligence that runs everything. It's like when you're connected to nature, connected to other people.

As the Bible says in 2 Corinthians 13:5, "Examine yourselves to see if your faith is genuine. Test yourselves. Surely you know that Jesus Christ is among you; if not, you have failed the test of genuine faith."

I have this belief that we are all one, that what affects you also affects me. So, when I'm helping one person, I'm also helping everyone else. When you have that mindset, you always want to do what's best, not just for yourself, but for others. This can serve as your guideline, your foundation.

CHAPTER 6

Employing the System to Scale Your Business

"My pitch to prospective agents is not just about the income. I explain to them that not only will they make more money, but they're also going to have more of an impact on people's finances."

— Hermie Bacus

Scaling your business makes more people successful

When someone uses my system, it's not just about making a lot of money by selling life insurance. I want partners. People who partner with me will end up doing a lot of good in this world. Life insurance is just the vehicle we use to make it happen.

My model is rare because I pour so much into people's growth and development. I want to help them grow as a person, as a leader, and as a businessperson. There are companies that invest in their employees, but not to this degree. It goes back to my core values, to my desire to help people.

I want them to be able to achieve success in the way *they* define it. That could be a high five-figure income. Or a six-figure income. For other people, this could mean freedom from the day-to-day grind of working for someone else.

Success for some people could mean working from any location they choose—the beach, the mountains, on location in Europe or South America. Others may be striving for the benefits a successful life insurance agency could afford them: sending their kids to college without incurring any debt, taking care of their elderly parents, or buying a new home or a new car. Still others may want a revenue stream that enables them to give to those in need.

I'm able to teach people to build and scale their businesses because I did the same thing with my life insurance agency. While I had been a successful real estate agent, I had no previous experience in the life insurance industry. Yet, despite that, I developed a system and, in my first 12 months in business, earned a revenue of $268,000. And each year, I've scaled my business, exponentially increasing my revenue.

Whenever I'm teaching my system, I'm making more people more successful.

Tracking your way to success

I'm a big believer in tracking your activities. I think the number one challenge with people who are in business is they have no system for tracking their activity. But tracking will help you stay focused.

I like to use a diamond system. On the left point of the diamond is "Belief." On the right is "Goal". This is because your goals have to be aligned with your beliefs. Then, at the bottom point is "Activity," because you need to know exactly what activities to complete to achieve your goals.

To be successful, your activity must align with the actions you're taking to achieve your goals. For example, many people will tell you they want to make $100,000 a year, but they have a habit of working minimum-wage jobs, so they're never going to achieve their goal if they're only working at the minimum wage level.

At the top of that diamond is "Results," which is what happens when your beliefs and goals are aligned, and you're working on the activities that will make those results possible.

There are five key metrics you need to track in this system.

1. Calls: the number of calls you need to make to get one appointment
2. Appointments: the number of appointments you need to set to get one person to show up for a presentation
3. Presentations: the number of presentations you must make to get one person to become a client
4. Closings: the number of clients you sign
5. Premium: the amount of money you make, on average, per client signed

By tracking these metrics, you can develop a ratio of success. Once you have the average premium, along with the average number of calls, appointments, presentations, and closings, you can predict your income.

For example, to get to $100,000 a year, you need X number of closings. To get that many closings, you need to make X number of appointments. And you keep working backward. So if, for example, it takes 10 calls to get one appointment and you want two appointments, then you know you need to make 20 calls. But we also may know that you need to make three appointments to actually get one person to show up. So, if one out of three people show up for their appointments and you want to present to two people, then you need to make six appointments, which means you've got to make 60 calls to get those appointments.

Calls	Booked Appointments	Actual Appointments with Potential Customers
60	6	2

By tracking your metrics, you can develop a ratio of success.

When you look at scaling your business, taking those numbers out further, if you want to present to five people in one week, you need to have 15 appointments scheduled. Now, if you make one sale for every three appointments and, for illustration, the average premium is $3,000 at a 70% rate, you're earning $2,100 income. This gives you a projection, and your income becomes predictable. Once you build your agency, if you have five agents under you and they average four or five sales a month, you'll know exactly the numbers they need to reach to achieve that number of sales.

Tracking your numbers gives visibility to everything you do. When I watch my agents with no experience look at their numbers in their first 90 days, they think they're terrible. A year later, when they compare the numbers from their one-year mark to their first 90 days, they get excited when they realize how much better they are.

The challenge people have in tracking their numbers is they're not used to it. To make it easier for them, we have an app that automatically does it for them. When they make a call, that's immediately recorded in the system.

This simple process makes it easier to scale your business.

Using the Builder's Quadrant to spend your time with the right people

Since we only have a set number of hours in the day, it's critical we spend our time with the people with whom we'll have the most impact.

I have a method called the Builder's Quadrant that helps me focus my time. It helps me establish who I should be spending more time with. It resembles the importance/urgency matrix from productivity but instead represents alignment and production.

I spend 75% of my time with people who are aligned with our vision and our core values but are not producing. I spend a lot of time coaching and mentoring them. The goal is to provide them with the skill set to become producers. These people are in the upper right quadrant, and I identify them as the Green Apples.

Since we only have a set number of hours in the day, it's critical we spend our time with the people with whom we'll have the most impact.

I spend 20% of my time with my top producers. They are already aligned with our core values and vision. Most of these people already know what to do, so I don't want to bother them. I have an open-door policy with them, and they'll come to me when they need me. I just make sure I'm available if and when they need me. This group is in the upper left quadrant and are the Red Apples.

The remaining 5% of my time is spent with agents who are producing but are not aligned, so they typically don't want to talk to me. They like the concept of what we're doing, and that's why they're producing. But when they have problems, they do call, which accounts for about 5% of my time. This group takes the lower left quadrant and is called Brown Apples.

The final group makes up the lower right quadrant and is called Rotten Apples. These are the people I don't want to spend time with because they're not aligned with the program, and they're not producing.

The Builder's Quadrant helps me focus my time.

For the Green Apples, I have twice-a-week training and mentoring sessions where they have access to me and can ask questions to help guide them through the steps. Through this, I provide them with the training and tools they need. Additionally, they can use an app that helps them go through the training in a step-by-step method. They also have access to my calendar, so they can set up an appointment with me.

I have a separate weekly session for the Red Apples, where I'm available if they need me. For this group, our sessions are typically focused on accountability. Then, of course, they can set an appointment with me if they need some help growing their business.

The training materials we use are different for each level.

When I teach people the scaling system, they understand they're prospecting for two types of people. First, they're prospecting for people who need life insurance, and second, for people who are looking for a better life and may want to join the program.

Often, the agent pool comes from the client base. We sometimes see one out of every five new clients sign up to become an agent.

But people still need to prospect beyond their client base to add to their team.

Pitching for new agents

When I'm looking for new agents, I always talk about leveraging time—and the value you place on things based on how long it took and how much it cost.

For example, I ask people if they'd rather spend five years in college and come out making $60,000 to $70,000 a year, or would they rather get trained in 90 days and make a six-figure income.

I went to college for four years, and my first full-time salary was $45,000. Conversely, in my first year in real estate, I made $60,000. In 2000, I made almost $100,000 as an engineer and $230,000 working part-time in real estate. I realized something was definitely wrong with that picture.

My pitch to prospective agents is not just about the income. I explain to them that, not only are they going to make more money, but they're also going to have more of an impact on people's finances.

While people talk about money, it's not really the money that makes them want to do the business.

When I first meet with a prospect, I start the conversation by talking about commitments. I want to know how much time they can dedicate to the business. I address their desire. I point out that this business is not as easy as most people think; that while it's good money, it does take a lot of work. The key is the amount of the time commitment they're going to make in the first 30 days, because that's going to make the difference in their growth. After the first 30 days, that's when they typically commit to the program, decide it's the career they want to have, and decide they're all-in on the program.

The second factor is to determine why they want to make that kind of money. I find that while people talk about money, it's not really the money that makes them want to do the business. So, we explore their whys. I also ask about their core values because I want to make sure this is a good fit for them. When I see there's an alignment with their core values and the vision, I'm going to start them with the process.

This process isn't a do-it-yourself, one-and-done type of deal. The reason my clients are so wildly successful in a short time frame is because of the mentorship that's built into the program. Chapter Seven discusses our mentorship methods further.

CHAPTER 7

The Mentoring System to Success

"Free mentoring is one of the benefits of joining our team."

— Hermie Bacus

Holistic mentoring expands beyond business mastery

People across the country are constantly seeking out mentors and coaches to help them along their business path. They spend thousands of dollars a year for this expertise. But that is just one of the benefits of joining our team: the training and mentoring we provide to help you achieve success in our program is free.

I have a vision of empowering others to live exemplary lives and a track record of helping them become financially successful. Mentoring helps them open up to new ideas.

The mentoring we do as part of our system uses a holistic approach. I don't focus just on business mastery; I cover the five Fs—faith, fitness, family, finance, and fun.

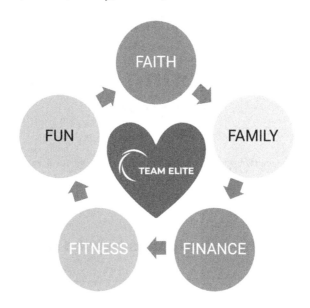

Faith

I start with faith because that's where our deep-seated beliefs lie. When I say faith, I'm not referring to religion, but instead a spiritual growth. Many people say they believe in something but don't follow or practice those beliefs. So, I'll talk about modeling what you believe.

Other people are held back because they don't know what they believe. They're just going through the motions and haven't taken the time to find out who they are and what they really want to be. So, they just buy into someone else's beliefs or choose to live their life based on someone else's expectations.

Originally, that had been my experience. For the longest time, I was trying to live my life based on my parents' expectations. That was holding me back.

I mentor based on faith, which is actually a quest for personal mastery. It's really about discovering yourself, finding out who you are and what you want.

Fitness

We cover both the physical and emotional aspects of fitness. We run several physical challenges, like a 66-Day Challenge and a Walk to Africa challenge. We have a First Friday Fitness challenge where the team will come together for a hike. We have a lot of activities like this that bring people together. But we're a nationwide organization, so for some activities, our people have to get out and do them on their own.

My mentorship program covers the five Fs—faith, fitness, family, finance, and fun.

Family

Our family mentorships are about relationships. So, your actual family is on top, but we're also talking about your friends, your team, and your clients. We hold a family barbecue every year where our team can invite their friends and clients. We do the same with team Christmas parties. These are big events for us because they're part of our mentoring program where you can build that relationship because, as we know, people only do business with people they know, like, and trust.

Finance

The finance portion of our mentorship is important because we're selling a financial product. For our finance mentorship, we're talking about leaving a legacy for your family and teaching people to save money. It's a little-known fact, but many financial advisors don't invest in their own products. We're not like that. We're teaching our agents that they need to leave a legacy. They're selling life insurance, so they should at least have an insurance policy for themselves. That's one of our mentoring principles: teaching our agents to make sure their families are protected. They need to start saving money.

We teach our agents the 70-10 formula. There are three 10s in this equation. The first 10% goes directly into your savings toward your retirement. The second 10% goes toward charity, while the third 10% is allocated for taxes. You've got to save that for taxes.

The bulk of your money—70%—is directed back into investing in your business. Whatever money you have left is for your personal expenses. I always tell people not to kill the golden goose because often, in a budget crunch, they'll reduce the business budget without touching their personal budget. Instead, they should keep their business budget intact and eliminate personal expenses by, for example, shutting off their cable. Those personal expenses aren't making you money, but your business budget will.

Fun

The fun category is more about our personal side. First, they should be someone that people want to be around because they're fun. Second, I want to tie fun into their goals. For example, if you want to buy a car, you should set a goal so you earn that car by completing your activities for a certain period of time. They could also set weekly goals. Say you want a massage every week, and you're supposed to make 50 calls a week. You earn your massage when you make all your calls. So, your fun activities become a reward for doing the things you need to do.

Kickstarting the day with the 6:15 Club

I run a mentoring group called the 6:15 Club. We meet twice a week, on Tuesdays and Thursdays, at 6:15 a.m. PT. It's a free 45-minute mentoring session and we rarely talk about business, but we do talk a lot about faith and about our personal development. We typically have about 120 people in attendance.

It's a great way for people to kick off their day and stay connected with the rest of the team.

Client success: mentoring his way to success

One of the people who joined my team was a car salesman. He had his back against the wall and needed to earn $100,000 in three months. He already had a license, but he didn't have a team. So, I showed him our system, and he followed the plan, carrying out the activities, bringing on agents, and training them in the proper way. In three months, he exceeded his goal and finished the quarter with $110,000.

He is a great example of the type of success people can achieve when they follow our system.

CHAPTER 8

How Giving Back is Instrumental to Your Business and Personal Development

"There's only two reasons people feel significant. One is personal growth and the other is contribution."

— Tony Robbins

Why giving back is so important

The ability to give back to people and to the community is incredibly important. I believe that unless you can celebrate someone else's success, it will be hard for you to be happy and successful.

As Tony Robbins says, there are only two reasons people feel significant. One is personal growth, and the other is contribution.

Giving back is so important because it makes you feel like you matter. My philosophy is that while success is great, what is the point of it if you don't share it? Seeing the impact of your success on other people's lives is a great thing.

Giving back can be what's in your heart, the people you want to help. Many people give back through their church. Charities can use help, not only financial assistance, but also volunteers, either generally or with specific skills. To bring it closer to home, you could help someone in your family or on your team become financially successful.

My professor's act of generosity towards me inspired me to have the type of impact I'm making with a lot of people today.

How someone giving back to me changed my life

When I came to the United States, I attended San Jose Bible College. Coming from the Philippines, attending college was expensive, and I didn't have much money.

One of my professors offered to pay my tuition. I had been working in the school's cafeteria and didn't have enough money. I probably wouldn't have been able to take classes the next semester because I couldn't afford the tuition. This professor approached me and offered to pay my tuition so I could stay in school.

I still remember his generosity because I feel that was my turning point. If he hadn't made that offer, I'd probably be in the Philippines today.

His unselfish act of generosity changed my life. He made a huge impact on me and the rest of my life. I don't think he even knows how important he is to me. Later, I tried to find him to thank him, but I couldn't. His act of generosity inspired me to have the type of impact I'm making with a lot of people today.

Who do you want to impact?

I always think about the impact we can make on people, even though we may never know the results of our actions.

I look at my story—that professor doesn't know his impact on me and the results of his act of kindness. But I know, and he was amazing. He was one of my favorite professors. For him, his generosity was probably just a natural act, but for me, it had a profound impact.

If we have that same mindset and help others when and how we can, we may never know the impact we can have. The chain effect of that one act of kindness could be the difference to hundreds, maybe thousands of people.

For example, our team gets involved in group givebacks. Since I'm from the Philippines, when there have been disasters there— floods or earthquakes—we've helped out. We've also gotten together to give money to people who have lost a family member but couldn't afford to go home to be with their loved ones.

The chain effect of one act of kindness could be the difference to hundreds, maybe thousands of people.

I look at giving back as part of an infinite cycle. It's the mindset that your success is someone else's success and, since we're all part of the same team, if we can't celebrate someone else's success, then we'll never be successful individually. This thinking puts you in a competition with yourself, not with someone else. It becomes a never-ending quest to be better—a better parent, a better person, and a better agent. It never ends, except that we just need to grow on a daily basis. If we can help each other grow, it creates an infinite cycle of giving back, where I'm helping you grow, and you're helping me grow; we're just helping each other.

This mindset of giving back helps us with new people in our organization who are going to need help, so we naturally give back to that person. It creates a culture where everyone has that winning mindset that never ends. It's infinite.

When I talk about giving back, it's not just in terms of charity, although that can be a piece of it. Instead, it's also about giving back to the team around you and helping them develop and grow.

When people have evidence of you giving back and helping others, they're more apt to model your behavior and start impacting others around them by also giving back.

Cultivating the tsunami effect to success

A giving-back mindset is integral to scaling up the business. Without it, you're not going to be excited about having to help all the people you're bringing into the organization.

I liken it to the effects of a tsunami that people will see five years from now. In the beginning, you have a lot of average people, and you're not getting big results. But because they're getting trained and getting the help they need, it will create a tsunami that, five years from now, will leave everyone wondering where all the results came from. Right now, you have a lot of people growing together, and suddenly, boom, you've got this huge force coming out. Just like a tsunami, most people will never see it coming.

A giving back success story

A woman joined our organization but wasn't very receptive in the beginning. She needed our environment to grow, but even though she was selling here and there, she wasn't really following the system. She was not a fast starter, and it took her 18 months before she did anything big.

When she adapted to our system after 18 months, it only took her an additional six months for her to make over $100,000. She hit the six-figure income mark for the next five years and was making $800,000 a year.

It was so satisfying for me to watch her evolution. And what was even better, in a one-year time span, she mentored someone else who went from $100,000 a year to making over $700,000.

The beauty of this system is that I can easily teach it to people who are willing to learn.

CHAPTER 9

Living the Producer's Lifestyle

"The Producer's Lifestyle gives you the freedom of autonomy. You have the opportunity to operate this business when and where you want."

— Hermie Bacus

When people follow my system, they can look forward to living the Producer's Lifestyle. This is a lifestyle that gives you the freedom of autonomy. You won't have to worry about anyone not approving of what you're doing, working on someone else's timeline, or how much it costs financially. You have the opportunity to operate this business when and where you want as long as you're following the system and completing the necessary activities to be successful.

Getting started in Year One

Your first year in our program is about survival. You're new, and you haven't yet established yourself in the business. You're probably going to get a lot of pushback and challenges from your family, friends, and peers, and you must overcome this.

During this time, you just want to show up, get your training and mentoring, and learn who we are because that's going to be the key. But whatever you do, you want to stick with it. You don't want to quit. You want to get to know the company and simply understand there will be a lot of challenges.

In your first three months, you'll go from getting licensed to getting trained to learning the system to building your agency.

You're making sales and bringing in a few agents.

When people first come on board, we give them a 90-day plan. During their first three months, they go from getting licensed to getting trained, to learning the system, to building their agency.

This 90-day window will give you an idea of whether this is the opportunity for you and whether you want to be part of our organization.

Year Two: shortening the learning curve

Once you put all the first-year challenges behind you, it's time to advance into year two. During the year's learning curve, you're getting a better grasp of the product, the system, the market, our compensation plan, and everything you need to be able to build your own agency and increase your business. During this time, you're earning while you're learning. This is when you start leading your people and modeling the activities and skills required to build a business.

In addition to any new sales you make, you're also signing renewals and getting a percentage from them. So, you now start to experience the residual part of the compensation. This is why it's so important people don't quit in the first year, because they'll never get to the good part, which is residual income.

Building your agency in Year Three

In the third year, you're building your agency. You're working to get it to the level you want it to be. During this time, you don't want to be comparing yourself to other people. Everybody is different, and the size of people's businesses will vary. You want to take it to a level where you feel comfortable and you can create passive income.

You're also leading people and modeling what it's like to build a business so your agents can grow their own.

The million-dollar year: Year Four

Although some people choose to stop at half a million dollars a year, for people who really work the system and continue to build their agency, your fourth year is when you have the potential to reach the million-dollar-a-year mark in passive income. While you still may write policies, most of your time in the business will now be spent on growing the team and developing leaders. You'll be able to enjoy the fruits of your labor. At this point, whatever your level of income, you'll be able to leverage time and do whatever you'd like.

For some people, this means a nice house. For others, it's driving a nice car. I know people who are driving Ferraris and Bentleys. Another benefit is being able to vacation anywhere you want at any time you want. For still others, it's doing all three things.

When you reach this level, you're having more fun and working with more capable leaders on your team.

Enjoying a business that runs on its own: Year Five

In the fifth year, your business practically runs itself and you can enjoy all the benefits of it. You're just multiplying your success, building upon your growth, and receiving more residuals. The leaders you've put in place underneath you are now training additional leaders below them until it gets to a point where you have a self-perpetuating system. It's in everyone's interest to raise up the leaders underneath them.

You now have a business that no longer requires your presence.

Personally, you have more options. This is when you can upscale the neighborhood you live in, go on nice vacations, and purchase multiple vacation homes.

At the end of year five, you can continue on your growth trajectory. You continue to apply my system and keep adding leaders and agents, selling more policies, and collecting a higher level of income. Your income stacks up year after year.

Through our system, you've achieved your definition of success. As we mentioned before, that definition varies by person, but you've attained the financial independence and income you sought and can now live the life many people only dream of.

CHAPTER 10

Get Started with Your 90-Day Business Plan

"You have it within your power to make your life a great story, one of significance."

— John Maxwell

As we mentioned in Chapter 2, it takes about 90 days to show success in your new business. If you follow our 90-day plan, you'll be well on your way to achieving success.

Setting goals and expectations

The most important thing to know about your life insurance business right from the start is that 90% of it is mental. Having the right mindset is crucial to your success. You must decide in advance that you're going to be successful. You also need to decide you're going to act in a professional manner. The remaining 10% of your business are the physical activities of taking action, recruiting, and working with prospects, customers, and agents.

In order to know if you've arrived at your destination and achieved the level of success you're striving for, you first need to know where you're going, why you're going there, and how you'll get there.

When your goals inspire you, when you believe and act on them, you will accomplish them.

This starts by establishing your goals. But these cannot be arbitrary. To have the best possible chance of achieving your goals, they must include three components. They must be:

- Inspiring
- Believable
- Something you can act on

When your goals inspire you, when you believe and act on them, you can accomplish them.

Start by listing three goals you'd like to achieve over the next 90 days. This could include the value of the policies you'd like to sell; the number of calls, appointments, and presentations you'll make; and the number of agents you sign. You'll want to make these goals believable. They shouldn't be so low they don't inspire you, but they also shouldn't be so high they're unattainable.

Next, you need to determine your motivation. As we discussed in Chapter 1, it's important you know your "why." This will help you get through the challenges that will come up along the way. List out three reasons why this is the business you want to pursue above all other opportunities. But, as you're doing this exercise, dive deep. Don't stop at the first thing that comes to mind. For example, if one of your whys is that you want to have more time to spend with your family, why is that important to you? What would you do with that additional time? How would that benefit you? Your spouse? Your kids? Your parents or siblings?

Complete that step with each of your whys. For example, if you want more income, why do you want more income? What would you do with that higher level of income? How would you spend it? Would you go on trips? Where would you go? What would you buy? A new house? New car? What type of car?

When you're identifying your whys and diving deep into those reasons, you're creating an internal vision board, a picture of what your life could look like when you achieve the success you're striving for. By painting this picture, you no longer have an abstract idea of what your life could be, but instead, something that seems real and could become real when you follow through with your actions.

Then, we move into the core values we discussed in Chapter 3. What is it that is important to you? Why is it important? Think about this in the areas of faith, fitness, family, finance, and fun. When you discover your core values, you'll learn if your activities support those values. This will help you on your business journey. So, jot down your top five core values.

But, as in the last exercise, go deep into your core values. If one of your core values is to be fit, what does that mean? Does that indicate a certain weight you want to attain? If so, what is that number? Why is that number important? Does it mean you want to exercise a certain number of times a week? Why? How many times? What are you trying to achieve through this exercise? What type of exercise? The more specific you can get in identifying and defining each of your five core values, the more real they become, and the more you'll be able to internalize and act on them.

When you've completed these activities, you can write your own story… in advance. Look into the future five years and see who you'll be and what you will have achieved. What do you want your family to say about you in five years? Create a portrait of the future that you're striving to attain. Again, make it specific and descriptive. Tell your future story in a way that comes to life, where you can see yourself in the starring role and know this is a life you could achieve by following and acting on the right system.

Track your way to success

As we discussed in Chapter 6, it's important to track your activities. This is the only way to tell if your activities are aligning with your goals.

Every week, you'll want to keep track of your engagements, confirmations, guests, recruits, and points. At the end of the week, assess your progress. What did you do well? What were your challenges? Why did you find those things challenging? What's the one thing you can do that will have the biggest impact the following week?

Only by tracking and measuring your activities will you know what you need to improve.

This starts by tracking your daily activities and seeing how they stack against your goal. How many engagements did you have each day? How many confirmations? What were your goals for those activities? Did you meet or surpass your goals? Or did you miss the mark by a little? Or a lot?

Incorporate your daily activity into your weekly results. For the week, how many guests did you have? How many recruits?

Then, check the ratio for your weekly activities. Compare:

- Engagements vs. Confirmations
- Confirmations vs. Guests
- Guests vs. Recruits

Only by tracking and measuring your activities will you know what you need to improve.

Schedule your way to success

One of the best ways to hold yourself accountable to your business and your success is to schedule and track your time. This includes all aspects of your life, both your personal life and your business-related activities. Schedule everything and prioritize your activities. On an hour-by-hour calendar that runs Monday through Sunday, block out time for the following:

- Family
- Exercise
- Prospecting/money-making activities
- Presentations
- Follow up
- Fast start training
- Corporate overview
- Agent training
- Underwriting response
- Coaching/mentoring
- Conventions

The best way to make sure you complete this activity is to do it at the same time every day. Try to schedule and accomplish this either first thing in the morning or at the end of your day.

Schedule all aspects of your life.

As you're scheduling your time, give special attention to money-making activities, such as:

- Prospecting/generating leads
- Converting leads/inviting people in
- One-on-one presentations
- Closing/asking for the order
- Following up
- Fast track training
- Corporate overview/agent training

Be careful you don't spend too much time on non-money-making activities, like:

- Underwriting requirements
- Training calls
- Talking to your downline/upline
- Attending meetings
- Buying/using product
- Understanding the compensation plan
- Mentoring with your upline
- Getting organized

The success compression

At its most basic, every day you want to work on prospecting for new customers and agents and scheduling presentations. Every week, work on recruiting and making sales. Every month, work on your business launch and fast-start promotion.

At the 90-day mark, you'll start duplicating your efforts to bring in more agents, more sales, and more success.

By following this plan, you can start living the life of your dreams and achieve the level of financial and personal success you set as your goal.

As John Maxwell said, "You have it within your power to make your life a great story, one of significance."

CONCLUSION

*"It is my goal to help people achieve financial freedom, and I
have found building and growing a life insurance agency is the
best method for most people to achieve that result."*

— Hermie Bacus

It's time to get started

Throughout this book, I have shown you my path to success—
how I went from a standard government job to a successful real
estate career that brought me a linear income to my current
profession, running FinFitLife, a life insurance agency that
has grown exponentially and brought me an untold amount of
wealth while giving me the opportunity to help people such
as yourself.

I've taken you through my process in a step-by-step manner,
demonstrating why running a life insurance agency is such a
fantastic business opportunity and giving you the mechanics
of how you can start and run a six- or seven-figure agency of
your own.

It is my goal to help people achieve financial freedom, and I
have found building and growing a life insurance agency is the
best method for most people to achieve that result.

I've already taken hundreds of people, who are now living their best lives, through this process. Now, I'd like to help you attain a life of financial freedom and your personal vision of success.

Why this may be the opportunity you've been looking for

You picked up this book and read it through to its completion because you have a burning desire to be an entrepreneur. You may have tried and not succeeded in the past, but you know, with the right opportunity and the right system, you could achieve success.

Even though you may be stuck in the 9 to 5 grind right now, continuing in a job that requires endless hours and answering to a boss is no longer appealing to you because you know there's a world of opportunity available once you find and act on the right opportunity.

So why is my system through FinFitLife the perfect opportunity for you? Let's take a look at...

What your new future looks like

What would it mean for you and your family if you earned a high five-figure income? Or a six-figure income? Continue that thought and picture your life with an annual seven-figure income!

Would you move? Into a new house in an upscale neighborhood? Buy new cars? Send your kids to college without the need for student loans? Go on exotic vacations? Multiple times a year?

What would it mean to you to not have to worry about paying your monthly bills? Instead of having a minimum amount left at the end of your paycheck, with our system, you could have a great deal of money left at the end of the month.

How would it feel to be able to support your parents and take away all their financial worries? How about your in-laws, too? Perhaps give your kids a financial jumpstart on their lives so they can start their own business?

This dream life is possible through our system, and you could join the ranks of people already enjoying the life that using our system has afforded them.

Throughout this book, I shared with you stories of some of the people who have gone through our system and the success they've achieved. Can you picture yourself in a similar story? Where I'm sharing the exponential success you've achieved?

These people have attained financial stability and financial freedom, and I want to share my system with you so you can also achieve your best life...your definition of success.

But if you don't take advantage of our system...

It's sad, but not everyone will take advantage of this amazing opportunity. For whatever reason, the roadblocks that have been holding them back will continue to stop them, and they'll decide they don't want to enjoy a life of luxury and all the finer things in life.

Instead, they may be stuck, constantly struggling in their current circumstances, working 9 to 5 or even more hours, worrying about house payments, car payments, credit card bills, student loan payments, and all the financial issues that crop up to cause stress and worry.

But you don't have to be one of those people. Instead, you can explore everything our system has to offer. We'll get you started with our 90-day success sprint, which will take you through the entire process of learning to run a life insurance agency: getting licensed and trained, building your agency, and adding independent agents.

By the end of those three months, you'll know for sure if this is the opportunity you've been dreaming of and seeking. You'll be able to get a vision of what your personal future could look like and the money and lifestyle you could achieve when you continue with our system.

Don't let fear or doubt hold you back. Take your future into your own hands and chart your own way through life. Simply scan the QR code to get started on this amazing, life-changing opportunity.

ABOUT THE AUTHOR

Hermie Bacus came from the Philippines in 1986 as an exchange student with a big dream. Working as a Civil Engineer in a City Government in Silicon Valley for 10 years and a successful 20 year real estate broker background, he shifted his career to Financial Services in April 2013.

Team ELITE (Empowered Leaders Influence Today's Entrepreneurs) was born when he embraced the journey to make a difference in people's lives. His "Value Driven" culture drives the Vision, Leadership and Success into new heights and has helped over 100 people make 6 to 7-figure income a year. Team ELITE is marked as the fastest growing team in the company earning a million dollars a year in just four years!

Success leaves clues! In this book, Hermie articulates how he did it. A lot of successful people are not willing to teach or can not articulate how they made it! Hermie is willing, can articulate, train and mentor you to duplicate what he did! Team ELITE is rising to the top because of so many leaders stepping up leading the way.

—

Made in the USA
Columbia, SC
09 November 2024

45798561R00065